Bones

Injury, Illness and Health

Carol Ballard

Heinemann
LIBRARY

www.heinemann.co.uk/library
Visit our website to find out more information about **Heinemann Library** books.
To order:
☎ Phone 44 (0) 1865 888066
▤ Send a fax to 44 (0) 1865 314091
▯ Visit the Heinemann Bookshop at www.heinemann.co.uk/library to browse our catalogue and order online.

First published in Great Britain by Heinemann Library, Halley Court, Jordan Hill, Oxford OX2 8EJ, part of Harcourt Education. Heinemann is a registered trademark of Harcourt Education Ltd.

Editorial: Nick Hunter and Catherine Clarke
Design: Jo Hinton-Malivoire and Tinstar Design Limited (www.tinstar.co.uk)
Illustrations: pp. 8, 21, 31, 32, 36, 41 by Geoff Ward; pp. 18, 19 by Ken Vail Graphic Design
Picture Research: Maria Joannou and Su Alexander
Production: Viv Hichens

Originated by Ambassador Litho Ltd
Printed and bound in China by South China Printing Company

ISBN 0 431 15714 6
07 06 05 04 03
10 9 8 7 6 5 4 3 2 1

British Library Cataloguing in Publication Data
Ballard, Carol
Bones. – (Body focus)
612.7'5
A full catalogue record for this book is available from the British Library.

Acknowledgements
The publishers would like to thank the following for permission to reproduce photographs: Corbis p. **7** (Kevin Fleming); Corbis Stockmarket pp. **22** (Tom and Dee Ann McCarthy), **25** (Lester Lefkowitz), **40** (Phillip Bailey); Imagestate p. **6**; Science Photo Library pp. **5** (Manfred Kage), **10**, **11** (BSIP, University of Zurich), **12** (Secchi-Lecaque, CNRI), **13** (Martin Dohrn), **14** (Department of Clinical Radiology, Salisbury District Hospital), **15** (Damien Lovegrove), **16** (Alfred Pasieka), **17** (Biophoto Associates), **20** (Peter Gardiner), **23** (Department of Radiology, Salisbury District Hospital), **26** (Dr P. Marazzi), **28** (Mike Devlin), **29** (Princess Margaret Rose Orthopaedic Hospital), **30**, **34** (Dr P. Marazzi), **35** (Princess Margaret Rose Orthopaedic Hospital), **37** (Dr P. Marazzi), **38** (Gusto), **39** (Mauro Fermariello), **42** (Manfred Kage).

Cover photograph of the bones in a healthy human foot reproduced with permission of Science Photo Library.

The publishers would like to thank David Wright for his assistance with the preparation of this book.

Every effort has been made to contact copyright holders of any material reproduced in this book. Any omissions will be rectified in subsequent printings if notice is given to the publishers.

CONTENTS

Words appearing in the text in bold, **like this**, are explained in the Glossary.

THE HUMAN SKELETON

The skeleton of bones provides a strong framework for the rest of the body. It defines our shape, protects important organs and allows us to move. It also plays an important role in blood cell production and in storing **minerals** and fats.

The skeleton of a newborn baby may contain as many as 300 bones, but many fuse (join together) during childhood. Most adults' skeletons have 206 bones. The bones range in size from the tiny, delicate **ossicles** of the ear to the long, strong **femur** of the thigh. There is also a wide range of bone shapes, including the long bones of the limbs, short bones of the wrist and ankle joints, flat bones of the skull and irregular bones of the spine and face. The size and shape of each bone reflects its function.

Support and movement

The spine provides a strong, upright central support. The shoulders are attached to the spine by strong muscles, and the pelvic girdle is attached directly to the spine. Arms are suspended from the shoulders and legs are suspended from the pelvic girdle. This arrangement defines our overall shape, and the movements that we can make. Bones protect delicate internal organs from injury. The skull protects the brain, the spine protects the **spinal cord**, the ribcage protects the heart and lungs and the pelvic girdle protects abdominal organs.

Muscles are attached to bones by strong **tendons**. When muscles contract, bones are pulled into new positions, allowing us to achieve a wide range of movements. Some movements are large, such as the movement of the femur when we stride, while others are small, such as the precise movements of a violinist's fingers.

Joints are the places where the ends of two bones meet. Your skeleton has more than 200 joints. Some joints, like your knees and elbows, allow the bones to move. Strong bands called **ligaments** hold these joints together, controlling the movement of the bones. Other joints, like those in your skull, are fixed, so the bones cannot move at all.

At the centre of some bones is spongy **tissue** called red **bone marrow** that produces some blood cells. Adult bones also contain yellow bone marrow tissue. If we eat more fat than our bodies need, the excess will be transported by the blood to places where it can be stored. Some fat will reach the yellow bone marrow where it may be stored, and then released when required by other parts of the body. Bone tissue stores minerals, especially calcium and phosphorus, which help to make the bones strong. When these minerals are needed, bones can release them into the bloodstream for transport to other parts of the body.

skull

clavicle

ribcage

scapula

spine

humerus

pelvic
girdle

ulna

radius

femur

tibia

fibula

This diagram shows the main bones of the human skeleton. You can see how the spine provides a central support for all the bones of the upper body, and the pelvic girdle acts as a frame from which the legs can move freely.

HEALTHY BONES

We all need to make sure that we look after our bones, as a strong, healthy skeleton is important if we are to lead active lives. The food that we eat and the amount of exercise we do can both affect our bones.

Diet

Our bones are made from the chemicals that we receive from our food. For bones to grow strong and healthy, we need to make sure that the food we eat provides all the chemicals that are needed by our bones.

Bones contain a lot of calcium and phosphorus so it is important that your diet contains plenty of these two **minerals**, especially while you are growing. Smaller amounts of other minerals such as fluoride, manganese, iron and magnesium are also needed. Good sources of calcium include dairy products, such as milk and cheese, leafy green vegetables, such as cabbage and spinach, shellfish and eggs. Foods rich in phosphorus include dairy products, meat, fish, beans, grains and eggs. These foods also contain plenty of the other minerals needed.

Some **vitamins** are essential for building strong bones. Vitamin D, found in fish oils, butter and eggs, and also formed by the action of sunlight on skin, is needed to help calcium build up in the bones. Vitamin C, found in most fruits and vegetables, but especially in citrus fruits such as oranges, also plays an important part in building up strong bones.

Dairy products are a good source of calcium, and contain phosphorus – also found in eggs. Calcium and phosphorus both help us to have healthy bones.

Exercise

When you exercise, your bones are made to move and support your body's weight. This helps them to become stronger as more minerals are accumulated. Being inactive can lead to bones becoming weaker, as minerals are lost and bone **tissue** is broken down. The main work our bones do is mechanical, being pulled by muscles when we move and supporting our body against the pull of gravity. Weight-bearing activities such as walking and moderate weight-lifting help to build and retain bone **mass**. It is important when you are a teenager to build up as much bone mass as you can. As people age, bone mass is lost and cannot be built up again – so the more you have to begin with, the better!

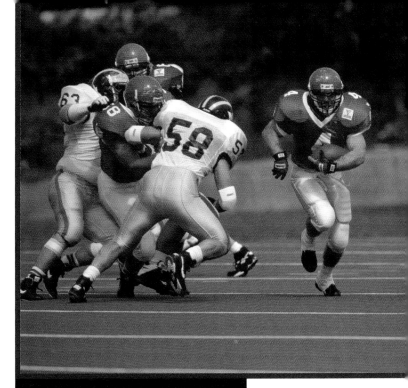

If you are playing a sport where you might injure a bone, try to protect yourself by wearing the correct protective clothing. These American footballers are unlikely to suffer damage beneath all this padding.

Astronauts and bones

Scientists have discovered just how important exercise is for healthy bones by studying what happens to the bones of astronauts who spend a long time in space. Without the pull of gravity, the human body is lighter – which means when exercising, the bones do not have to work so hard. The bones begin to lose calcium and other minerals, and even taking extra minerals as tablets cannot make up for this.

Protection

Bones can repair themselves, but it makes much more sense to avoid damaging them in the first place! Many sports activities have protective clothing specially designed to protect bones – shin pads for hockey and football; helmets for cycling, horse riding and mountaineering; elbowpads and kneepads for inline skating; arm guards and pads for cricket. American footballers are extremely well padded and protected.

TYPES OF BONE

The shape and size of bones varies, depending on their functions within the body. Large, strong bones like the thigh bone are needed for supporting the weight of the body, while smaller, delicate bones such as the **ossicles** inside the ear carry out tiny, precise movements. Bones are usually grouped according to their shape.

Long bones

Long bones have a greater length than width. They usually have a slight curve that makes them stronger than they would be if they were perfectly straight. There are special places on the long bones where muscles are attached. The bones act as levers, and move when they

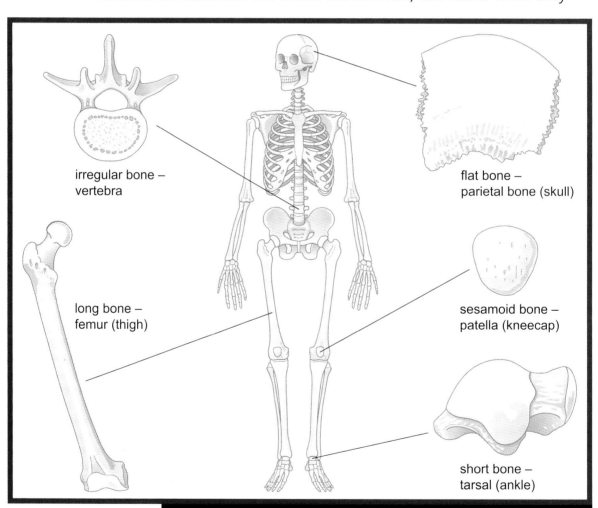

irregular bone –
vertebra

flat bone –
parietal bone (skull)

long bone –
femur (thigh)

sesamoid bone –
patella (kneecap)

short bone –
tarsal (ankle)

These diagrams show some of the main types of bone that make up the human skeleton.

The femur is a long bone. It needs to be strong as it supports the weight of most of the body when we walk or run. Short bones are found in ankle joints. The parietal bone is a flat bone.

are pulled by the contraction of muscles. The **femur** (thigh bone) and humerus (upper arm bone) are examples of long bones.

Short bones
Short bones are roughly cube-shaped, with their length, width and height being almost equal. Carpals are short bones found in the joints of the wrists, and tarsals are short bones found in the joints of the ankles. These bones allow flexibility as they slide easily past each other.

Flat bones
Flat bones are thin, curved and strong. Their strength makes them ideal for forming spaces to protect organs. Examples of flat bones are the ribs, scapula (shoulder blade), sternum (breastbone) and some bones of the skull.

Irregular bones
Irregular bones are complex shapes that do not fit into any of the other groups. The **vertebrae** and facial bones are all irregular bones. They have strange bits jutting out from them that allow them to connect with muscles and other bones.

Sesamoid bones
Sesamoid bones get their name because they are the shape of sesame seeds, although they are a lot bigger. They are found in joints where there is **friction** and tension between **tendons** and bones, such as the palms of the hands and soles of the feet. The number of these small bones varies from person to person, but everybody has the two large sesamoid bones that we call the kneecaps (patellae).

Accessory bones
Accessory bones are small, extra bones that occur in some people, most often in the feet. They arise when developing bones do not fuse (join together) completely to make a single bone, and so they can look like broken bones on X-rays. This can make it very difficult for doctors to accurately diagnose injuries to bones in the feet. Sutural bones are accessory bones found between the joints of the bones in the skull. When a baby is born, the skull bones are separate, like jigsaw pieces that are not fully locked together. As the baby grows, these bones slowly fuse to make the strong dome that we call the **cranium**. The joins between the bones are called sutures, and small sutural bones may be present between the sutures. Because the skull bones do not always fuse together in exactly the same way, the number of sutural bones can vary from one person to another.

BONE STRUCTURE AND COMPOSITION

Bones are not simple solids. They are made of living **tissue** arranged into several different layers with nerves and a blood supply. Their structure gives them strength, while keeping them as light as possible.

This X-ray shows the two long bones of the lower leg – the tibia and fibula.

Approximately 70 per cent of bone material is made up of different **minerals**, including calcium phosphate and calcium carbonate. The rest of the bone material is a network of living fibres and bone cells. It is the mineral content of the bone that makes it **rigid**. A baby's bones are quite soft and young children's bones are still slightly flexible. As a person grows older and more calcium, from the food they eat, is added to the bone structure the bones slowly become more rigid.

Types of bone cells

There are three main types of bone cell:
* **osteocytes** transport nutrients, waste and gases to and from the blood vessels
* **osteoblasts** make new bone tissue so that bones can grow and damage can be repaired
* **osteoclasts** break down old bone tissue to release minerals.

The actions of these cells are finely balanced. To maintain healthy bones, it is important that bone tissue is not broken down faster than new bone is produced.

Inside bones

If you look at the inside of a long bone such as the **femur**, you can see several different areas. The long, cylindrical central part is the shaft (diaphysis). At each end of the shaft is a growth plate, where osteoblasts make new bone tissue, making the bone grow longer. The outer ends of the bone are covered in a layer of smooth **cartilage**, to allow the bone to move freely at the joint.

The outer covering of a bone, the periosteum, is a tough, fibrous **membrane**. It contains osteoblasts, and blood vessels and nerves run through it.

Spongy bone has a mesh-like structure that makes it strong and supportive.

Inside the periosteum is a layer of dense, compact bone similar to the ivory of elephants' tusks. It is a network of bony columns, arranged around central canals through which arteries and veins run.

The centre of a bone is a light material called **spongy bone** (cancellous bone), arranged as a network of thin bars. These run in many different directions, forming a 3-Dimensional mesh. The large spaces between the bars may be filled with jelly-like material called **bone marrow**. Red bone marrow is found at the ends of long bones such as the femur (thigh bone) and is involved in the production of red blood cells. Yellow bone marrow fills the spaces in the shafts of long bones, and is mainly fat.

The internal structures of most bones are basically similar, but there are some differences. In some skull bones, there is no spongy bone, just a series of air spaces (**sinuses**), and the flat bones of the **cranium** have two thin plates of compact bone, with spongy bone sandwiched between them. Irregular bones and short bones have varying amounts of spongy and compact bone.

Red **bone marrow** produces all the red blood cells and some of the white blood cells in the body. Yellow bone marrow is mainly made up of fat cells. When a baby is born, all the bones contain red marrow. By the time they are six or seven years old, some of the red marrow becomes yellow marrow. This process continues, and in most adults red marrow is found only at the ends of the long bones such as the **femur**, in flat bones such as the ribs and sternum, and in the pelvic girdle.

Blood cell production

Blood cells age and are broken down, so new ones have to be made continually to replace them. The red bone marrow contains special 'stem' cells from which all the different types of blood cells can be made. The stem cells are like blank cells. As they grow and divide, they change and develop, becoming more and more specialized at each stage, until they eventually become new blood cells. Both white blood cells, which are involved in the body's **immune system**, and red blood cells, which transport oxygen around the body, are produced by bone

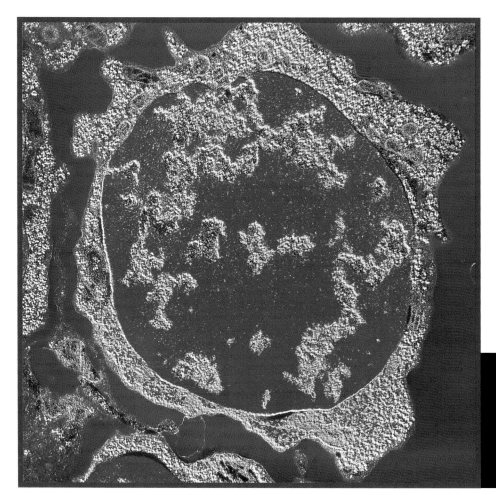

This picture shows a forming red blood cell from the human bone marrow.

In this picture, the red areas show some of the places where red bone marrow is located in adults.

marrow. Red blood cells only live for about 120 days. Healthy adults have about 250 million red blood cells in every drop of blood. To keep them at this concentration the bone marrow has to produce at least 2 million new red blood cells every second!

Control of blood cell production

Blood cell production is controlled by a feedback loop. Red blood cells carry oxygen around the body. If there are too few red blood cells, the level of oxygen in the blood drops. The kidneys detect this, and release a **hormone** called erythropoietin. This travels round the body in the blood, and when it reaches the bone marrow it speeds up the production of red blood cells. When the oxygen level gets back to normal, the kidneys stop releasing erythropoietin and red blood cell production slows down again.

Bone marrow problems

There are a number of possible reasons why bone marrow may not produce blood cells properly:
• some children are born with defective bone marrow
• chemicals, such as lead (found in water in buildings with old lead pipes, and in the air in areas with high levels of air pollution), benzene (found in some dyes and fuels) and arsenic (a poisonous chemical sometimes used in pesticides) can damage bone marrow
• X-rays and other types of radiation damage bone marrow
• some types of leukaemia, a bone marrow disease, can clog up the bone marrow with malformed white blood cells.

A bone marrow transplant can help in some of these cases. Red bone marrow from a healthy donor is injected into the blood stream of the patient. The stem cells travel around in the blood until they reach the patient's bone marrow. They settle there, and begin to produce healthy blood cells.

BROKEN BONES

Bones are strong – but an accident such as an awkward fall can break them. The medical term for a broken bone is a **fracture**. Some are simple and mend easily, while others are more complicated and may need surgery to help to repair them.

Type of fracture	What happens to the bone?
greenstick fracture	This occurs in young children. Their bones are more flexible than adults' bones, so although one side of the bone may be broken, the other side may simply bend a little.
partial fracture	The bone does not break completely into separate pieces. This is also called an incomplete fracture.
stress	This may be a single crack or a mass of many tiny cracks in the bone, without any other damage.
chip	A small piece of bone breaks off the main bone.
simple fracture	The bone snaps into two pieces, but they stay in line with each other.
compound fracture	This is like a simple fracture, but one or both of the broken ends of the bone stick right out through the skin.
comminuted fracture	The bone breaks into two, and part of it is shattered into smaller fragments.
impacted fracture	The bone breaks into two pieces and one is forced a little way inside the other.

This X-ray is showing a multiple fracture to the lower leg. Both the tibia and fibula have been broken.

Sporting fractures

The most common sporting fracture is of the collarbone (clavicle). This can get damaged as the result of a clumsy fall – landing on an arm stretched out to save yourself can put huge pressure on the collarbone, snapping it in two.

Stress fractures, usually of the shin bones, are the result of an action being repeated over and over again, such as the thumping of feet on a hard track by runners and jumpers. Wearing training shoes with good support can help to prevent stress fractures.

Treating fractures

To prevent any further damage, broken bones need to be kept as still as possible. A sling can support a broken arm, and **splints** can keep a broken leg rigid. X-rays give accurate information about the fracture. If it is a simple fracture, wet plaster bandage is wrapped around the bone, drying and hardening to form a protective shell. Bones that have moved out of alignment need to be repositioned, and some complicated fractures may need surgery to insert metal pins for extra strength.

How bones heal

When a bone is broken, red blood cells pour out from the damaged blood vessels, forming a blood clot at the site of the break. Tiny blood vessels called capillaries slowly grow into the clot, and dead and damaged bone **tissue** is removed by white blood cells and **osteoclasts**. Strong fibres form, connecting the ends of the bone. **Cartilage** forms in between, and gradually **osteoblasts** make new **spongy bone** tissue. Compact bone then forms around the new spongy bone. This whole process may take several months.

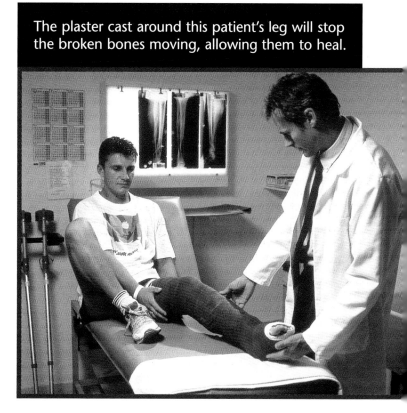

The plaster cast around this patient's leg will stop the broken bones moving, allowing them to heal.

BONE DISEASES

Although our bones are usually strong and healthy, there are various diseases that can affect them. Some are more serious than others. Different diseases affect people of different ages and have different causes, and therefore different treatments are required.

This colour X-ray shows the upper part of the femur, affected by osteoporosis. The parts coloured yellow-orange are fractures.

Osteoporosis

Osteoporosis is the weakening of bones as we age. The amount of **minerals** in our bones gradually decreases, and bone **tissue** is broken down more quickly than new tissue is made. The bars of the **spongy bone** become weakened, making the bones brittle and more likely to break easily. **Fractures** can occur just from normal activities – we may say an older person has fallen and broken a hip, but it would often be more accurate to say that their hip bone fractured and caused them to fall. Osteoporosis is a painful condition, also causing shrinkage and hunching of the backbone.

Osteoporosis causes more problems in women than in men, as the process of bone breakdown begins much earlier in women. In women, osteoporosis can start sometime after the age of 30, and accelerate in later middle age as **hormone** levels decrease. Hormones help to maintain bone strength. As hormone levels remain at a higher level for longer in men than in women, osteoporosis does not usually begin in men until after the age of 60. Hormone replacement therapy (HRT) and calcium supplements can help to prevent osteoporosis. A diet rich in **vitamins** and **minerals**, particularly calcium and phosphorus can reduce the risk of developing osteoporosis. Weight-bearing exercise, such as walking, also plays an important role by stimulating more new bone tissue to be made.

Osteomyelitis

Bones can be infected by **micro-organisms** such as *Streptococcus aureus*. **Bacteria** can get into the bone from outside the body, when a bone is broken, or from a wound or surgery. They can also spread inside the body from other infected places such as abscesses in the teeth. Infections in bones (osteomyelitis) causes fever, sweating and sickness. There may be pus and swelling at the site of infection. Osteomyelitis is usually treated successfully with **antibiotics**.

Rickets and osteomalacia

Vitamin D is needed for calcium to be able to accumulate in bones as they grow. Without vitamin D, calcium does not accumulate and the bones become soft and rubbery. This is called rickets, a disease in which children's bones are too weak to grow properly. The leg bones are not strong enough to carry the weight of the body, and so they are bent and bowed. Rickets is much less common in developed countries than it was in the past because diet and living conditions have greatly improved. In adults, lack of vitamin D prevents new bone tissue being made, and the bones feel painful and tender. This is adult rickets, also called osteomalacia.

This X-ray shows the bending of the leg bones that is typical in a child suffering from rickets.

Bone tumours

Bones may have odd lumps that do no harm at all, but **tumours** can also arise in bones. Although all bone tumours need to be investigated and treated, many are not **cancerous**. Osteosarcomas are the most common type of bone cancer, and, although they may affect older people, they usually occur in people between 10 and 20 years old. They can occur in any part of the body, but are usually found at the ends of the leg bones or ribs. The area may be painful, but often there are no symptoms and the disease may only be discovered when the bone breaks at the site of the tumour.

Osteosarcomas can be removed surgically, and then the patient usually receives chemotherapy (drug treatment) to kill any remaining tumour cells. Recent advances in treatment mean that these tumours can now usually be completely cured.

Inherited diseases

Some children are born with 'brittle bone disease' (*osteogenesis imperfecta*). The bones do not contain enough **proteins** and minerals so they are very weak and snap easily. Some babies even have broken bones when they are born. These children need to be very careful, and protected from any situations where the bones may be put under strain. This means they are very limited in what they can do, but as they grow older, the bones gradually get stronger so they are more able to lead a normal, active life.

Joints are the places where two bones meet. They allow the bones to move freely past each other, so that we can move all the parts of our bodies. Different types of joints allow different movements. There are two main types of joint in the human skeleton: hinge joints and ball and socket joints.

Hinge joints

These work like the hinge of a door, allowing movement in one direction – you can move a door backwards and forwards, but you can't move it up and down or round and round. The elbow joint is a hinge joint: if you keep your upper arm completely still, you can move your lower arm up and down but you can't wiggle it from side to side or move it round in a circle. The knee is also a hinge joint.

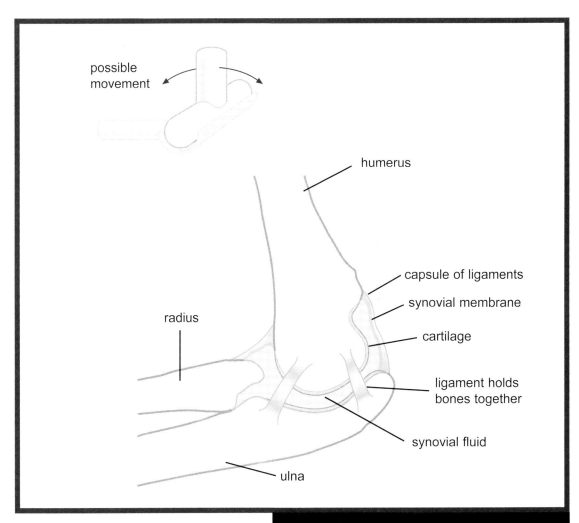

The hinge joint of the elbow allows the lower arm to move up and down.

Ball and socket joints

These allow a much wider range of movements than hinge joints. The end of one bone is a round lump (the ball), that fits snugly into a curved space (the socket) in the other bone. The shoulder joint, where the end of the humerus fits into the shoulder blade, is a ball and socket joint. Because of its design, you have a full range of movements – you can move your upper arm in just about any direction you want to.

The other major ball and socket joint is the hip joint, where the ball of the **femur** fits into the socket of the **pelvic girdle**. Although the bones could move very freely, tough bands of fibres limit their movements so for most people the hip joint has a smaller range of movements than the shoulder joint.

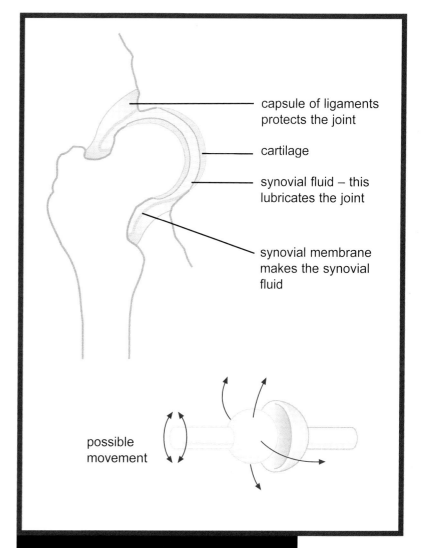

capsule of ligaments protects the joint

cartilage

synovial fluid – this lubricates the joint

synovial membrane makes the synovial fluid

possible movement

The ball and socket joint of the shoulder allows the upper arm to move freely in any direction.

Other joints

Not all our joints follow these two designs. Other types of joint include:
- fixed joints found between the bones of the skull. They are knitted tightly together, and allow no movement
- gliding joints of the wrist and ankle allow one bone to glide smoothly over the surface of another
- condyloid joints of the wrist and knuckles allow movement up and down, and from side to side
- saddle joints between the thumb bone and the wrist bones allow the thumb to move in all directions
- pivot joints allow a rotating movement of one bone around part of another. This type of joint in the neck allows us to turn our head from side to side: the top, ring-shaped **vertebra** balances on a point of the second vertebra.

Even the smallest joints are complex constructions. Structures are needed to keep the bones in place, to prevent the ends of the bones being damaged and to ensure that movements are smooth.

Fixed joints

In some fixed joints, bones are knitted together tightly by strong fibres, preventing movement. These are found between the bones of the skull.

Joints can also be held tightly together by pieces of **cartilage**. These can be found at the joint between the first rib and the **sternum**, and also where bones join at the front of the **pelvic girdle**.

Moving joints

Joints that allow bone movement have a more complex structure than fixed joints, and are called 'synovial joints'. The ends of each bone are covered with a layer of smooth cartilage, to reduce **friction** between them as they move past each other. The cartilage also acts as a cushion, absorbing shock.

This diagram shows the structures inside a synovial joint, in this case, the knee joint. You can see how the space between the bones is filled with synovial fluid (blue).

The whole joint is surrounded by the articular capsule, a sleeve-like cover that links the bones together. The outer layer of the capsule is made of tough fibres, which are flexible enough to allow movement, but difficult to stretch, to prevent the bones moving out of position. The inner layer, the synovial **membrane**, makes a liquid called synovial fluid. This fluid fills the space between the bones, the synovial cavity, and lubricates the inside surfaces of the joint.

Ligaments

Ligaments are tough bands of fibre that hold the joint together. They are really part of the articular capsule, and are very strong to prevent the joint being strained. Some ligaments are tiny, but some are much larger and have their own names. The hip joint has to take the full weight of the body, so the ligaments that hold the ball of the **femur** in the socket of the pelvis are extremely strong.

Extra structures

As well as the major structures of synovial joints, some contain additional structures. Extra bands called accessory ligaments can help to hold a joint together and are important in the knee joint. Some joints have small fluid-filled sacs or pads called **bursae** to act as a cushion when a **tendon**, muscle or skin may rub over a bone.

Some synovial membranes contain fat pads, as in the knee joint. Discs of cartilage may lie between the bones, attached to the articular capsule, and help to maintain the stability of the joint.

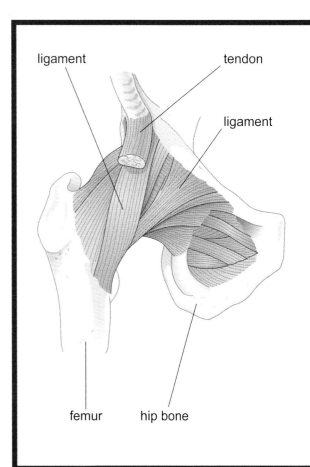

This diagram shows some of the ligaments that hold the hip joint together.

Joints are complicated structures, allowing us to move our bodies in many different ways. They are designed to be strong and stand up to normal wear and tear – but moving bones too far, too fast or in the wrong direction can damage the joints and cause a variety of injuries.

This doctor and athlete are looking at an X-ray of the athlete's knee injury and discussing possible treatments.

Sprain

Sprains are common injuries, caused by wrenching or twisting a joint too far. When the **ligaments** are over-stressed, they become stretched or even torn. The joint may swell, and a bruise may develop as blood leaks out of damaged blood vessels around the injury. Sprains can be very painful, but treatment with an ice pack can help to reduce swelling. Sprains usually heal well if the joint is rested and not put under further stress for a while.

You are more likely to sprain an ankle than any other joint – most people walk and run often and it is easy to miss your footing or trip on uneven ground, twisting the ankle and spraining it.

Dislocation

Dislocation occurs when the two bones of a joint become separated. The joint that is most commonly dislocated is the shoulder, as the head of the **humerus** moves out of the socket of the shoulder blade. Usually the humerus moves in front of the shoulder blade, rather than behind it.

This injury can be the result of an awkward fall, often in a physical sport such as football. Skilled medical staff can manipulate the joint and push the humerus back into its correct position. An X-ray may be taken to make sure that there are no **fractures**. After dislocation, it is very important to rest the joint in order to give it a chance to heal fully.

This diagram shows what happens when an elbow joint is dislocated.

Inflammation

Repeated, vigorous movements can lead to **inflammation** of the **bursae** inside a joint. The joint can become swollen as fluid collects inside it, and movement may be painful and limited. Injuries of this sort were often given names that reflected the type of activity that caused them, for example, 'housemaid's knee' as the result of kneeling for long periods and 'tennis elbow' resulting from over-use of the elbow joint.

Injuries like this will heal naturally if the joint is rested. An ice pack can help the inflammation to subside, and anti-inflammatory injections may also help. The extra fluid will slowly drain away and the swelling will go down so that movement is possible again.

Joint injuries and sport

Injuries to joints can prevent sporting activities for a while. However frustrating it may be, it makes sense to follow the doctor's advice and not start training again too soon, in order to give the joint time to heal properly. Stretched and torn ligaments take time to heal, dislocated bones need time to settle back into place and for any damaged tissue to heal, and inflammation takes time to subside. If you are impatient and use the joint again too soon, you risk aggravating the injury and needing even more time away from training.

KNEE INJURIES

The knee joint is the largest and most complex joint in the body. It is designed to allow the leg to bend, but it also needs to be **rigid** enough to hold the body stable when we stand still. It can be injured in a variety of ways, and damage can involve the bones themselves, the **ligaments**, **cartilage** and **tendons** of muscles.

The knee joint

Three bones meet at the knee joint – the **femur**, **tibia** and patella. Ligaments also link the **fibula** to the knee joint. The end of each bone is covered with a protective layer of cartilage. Pads of cartilage lie between the bones, acting as shock absorbers. Several **bursae** also cushion the knee joint.

Four strong ligaments bind the bones together:
- two cruciate ligaments make an X-shape as they cross over each other
- two collateral ligaments run down the sides of the knee joint

The patella is held in place in front of the end of the femur.

Torn cartilage

The pads of cartilage inside the joint may be damaged if the knee receives a direct blow, or is twisted awkwardly. If cartilage becomes wedged between the bones, the joint may 'lock' and cause a lot of pain. Doctors may remove small pieces of cartilage that have broken off the main cartilage or, if the cartilage is badly damaged, remove it entirely.

Torn ligaments

Ligaments may be torn by sudden twisting or by a direct blow, as in a rugby or hockey tackle. The person may hear a 'popping' sound, and the leg may buckle under their weight.

Inside knees

Until recent years, doctors had no easy way of finding out the extent of damage that may have occurred inside a knee joint. In the 1970s, Japanese surgeons developed the arthroscope, a small, illuminated tube that can be inserted into the knee through a small cut. This provides a clear view of the inside of the knee, sending detailed pictures to a monitor. Doctors can also now use microsurgical operating techniques, often needing a cut less than 1 centimetre long and requiring just a single stitch! This means that the recovery time from knee operations is much, much shorter than it used to be.

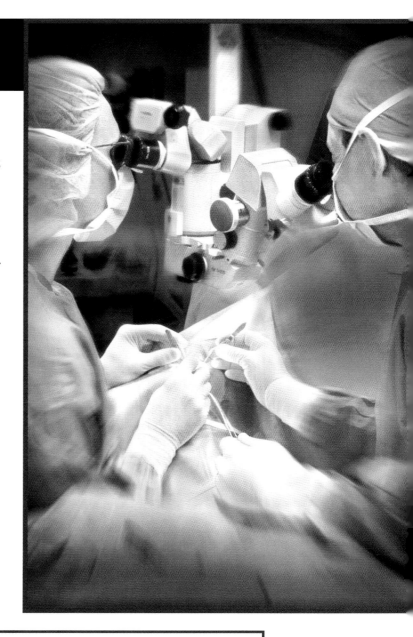

This picture shows a surgeon operating on a patient's knee.

If the ligament is damaged but not completely torn, a protective brace may be worn and exercises prescribed to strengthen the surrounding muscles.

If the ligament is completely torn, it can be repaired surgically. Collateral ligaments can be re-attached to the bones. Cruciate ligaments can be attached to sutures, (strong threads) that are then threaded through specially drilled holes in the femur, and the ends tied to hold them in place. Doctors may also use pieces of ligament from elsewhere in the body to help them repair these ligaments. Research is being conducted to try to find the best material to make artificial ligaments; several have been tried, including Gore-Tex, Dacron and carbon fibre, but with very limited success.

'Runner's knee'

This is one of the most common knee problems for runners, especially those who run long distances or on hills. It may be caused by always walking or running on the same side of the road: roads slope down a little at the sides, so unless you change sides one knee is constantly stretched more than the other. In normal movement, the patella slides backwards and forwards. In 'runner's knee' it also moves sideways a little as well, causing aching and tenderness underneath the patella. The pain usually gets worse when the person walks down stairs or squats down. Rest, and use of a brace, may help to relieve the condition.

Arthritis is the name given to painful, swollen joints. It can have many different causes but in most cases arthritis falls into one of two main types.

Osteoarthritis

Osteoarthritis is caused by the **cartilage** at the end of the joints wearing away. When you move your joints, the cartilage at the end of the bones is worn. Normally, the body replaces the cartilage, but sometimes it is worn away more quickly than the body can replace it. Eventually the bone surfaces become exposed and the joint becomes very painful. Large weight-bearing joints like the hip and knee are particularly likely to be affected.

Rheumatoid arthritis

While osteoarthritis is a result of wear on the joints, the causes of rheumatoid arthritis are more complex. It is probably caused by an 'autoimmune response'. This means that the body's **immune system**, instead of attacking germs from outside the body, attacks its own tissue, in this case the synovial **membrane** in the body's joints. The cartilage becomes very soft and wears away quickly in many joints at the same time.

Who is affected?

Many people believe that only older people are affected by arthritis, but this is not strictly true. Osteoarthritis does seem to be a natural product of the aging process but there are other causes too. Research has suggested that arthritis may be linked to certain **genes**, meaning that some people are born with a higher risk of suffering from arthritis than others.

This photograph shows the typical damage caused by arthritis. Standing and walking must be very painful for this person.

Rheumatoid arthritis, on the other hand, normally starts to show itself between the ages of 20 and 50, with women more likely to be affected than men. There is even a form of rheumatoid arthritis that appears in very young children, between the ages of two and five.

Dealing with arthritis

In most cases, treatment of arthritis is done by relieving the symptoms, for example through anti-inflammatory drugs that reduce the **inflammation** inside the joints. Medication is normally part of a three-step treatment that includes rest, to allow joints to reduce inflammation, and exercises, to rebuild strength in the joint. **Occupational therapists** can also help people to find easier ways of doing normal activities, avoiding the use of painful joints. In extreme cases of arthritis, doctors can sometimes replace the affected joints.

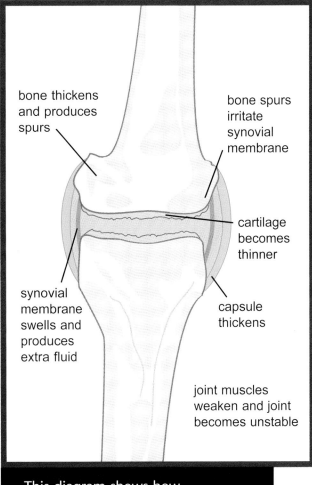

bone thickens and produces spurs

bone spurs irritate synovial membrane

cartilage becomes thinner

synovial membrane swells and produces extra fluid

capsule thickens

joint muscles weaken and joint becomes unstable

This diagram shows how osteoarthritis affects a knee joint.

Gold cure?

In the early part of the 20th century, scientists discovered that compounds of gold, whether swallowed or injected, could block the immune system and therefore be an effective treatment for rheumatoid arthritis. However, this treatment has harmful side effects, affecting the kidneys, and is now used with great caution.

Arthritis and sport

Osteoarthritis can affect younger people, especially if joints are over-exercised. There are cases of professional sportspeople who have suffered from the condition because they have continued to play on when injured. Anaesthetic sprays and creams prevent messages travelling from sensory receptors to the brain. This takes away the immediate pain of an injury so the person can continue to play – but the injury itself may actually be getting worse and worse. Use of **steroids** has also been linked to the development of arthritis at a young age.

JOINT REPLACEMENTS

Modern advances in medicine allow doctors to replace some damaged and worn out joints with artificial ones. This gives the patient freedom from pain and allows them to live more active lives than they would otherwise be able to.

Damaged joints

The most common reason for replacement of a joint is osteoarthritis. The **cartilage** covering the ends of the bones wears away, causing pain when the joint is moved as the bones rub against each other. The most common joint to be replaced is the hip joint. Knees are less commonly replaced and although shoulders can also be replaced, it is a relatively unusual operation.

This picture shows an artificial hip joint. The long shaft is inserted into a hole in the femur, and the socket is attached to the pelvis.

History

Doctors have tried for many years to find a way of replacing damaged and worn out joints. Some of the first experiments were carried out in the 18th century by German doctors using ivory, but these were not successful. In the 20th century, more attempts were made, and eventually a breakthrough was made in the late 1960s by a British **orthopaedic** surgeon, Sir John Charnley. He designed and used a metal ball and a plastic socket for a new hip joint, cementing the pieces in place with a plastic cement that was usually used by dentists. After his pioneering work, many other surgeons refined and perfected the techniques, and now more than 80,000 hip joints are replaced every year in the USA alone.

New developments

Alongside the developments in surgical techniques used in joint replacement have been developments in the materials used for the replacement parts. Some surgeons now use the metal titanium for parts of the new joints. Titanium is more flexible, and can support even greater loads than the natural bone. Another new development is an artificial knee joint covered with beads of cobalt. These beads encourage new bone material to grow over the joint, making it stronger and more permanent than just using cement.

Replacing a hip joint

There are two parts to the operation to replace a hip joint – attaching the new 'ball' to the **femur**, and replacing the socket of the **pelvic girdle**. Doctors first **dislocate** the hip, so that they can work on the joint. The top of the femur is removed, and the socket in the pelvis is carved out until it is exactly the right shape to hold the new shell. Once the shape is right, the shell may be held in place by the tightness of the fit, by screws, or by special cement. A hole is then drilled into the femur, and the shaft that holds the new ball is inserted. This too can be held by fitting tightly, screws or cement. The metal ball is attached to the shaft and the joint reassembled.

After an operation

Patients are usually encouraged to start moving around again soon after a joint replacement. Doctors may use a CPM (constant passive motion) device after a knee replacement. This motorized apparatus moves the joint continuously, even while the patient is asleep, without requiring any effort from the patient. Use of CPM can speed up the healing process considerably.

The full range of movement may not be possible with a replacement joint, but there is usually more movement and less pain than with a severely arthritic joint. Patients are advised to carry on with as many normal everyday activities as they can, but to avoid vigorous sports such as tennis and jogging.

Most replacement hips, knees and shoulders last for 10 to 15 years. Gradually, the parts wear loose in the bones, and this causes pain as the person moves. Another operation is then needed – either to insert another replacement joint, or to modify the existing joint to make it fit more tightly into the bone.

This X-ray shows the leg bones with an artificial knee joint in place.

The spine, or vertebral column, provides an upright support for the upper body. It is made up of a stack of small bones, the **vertebrae**, piled one on top of another. The bony canal that runs through the vertebrae provides a protective tube for the nerves of the **spinal cord**.

The vertebral column contains 33 vertebrae, some of which are fused together. Each single vertebra is a very slightly different shape from the ones above and below, so they fit together to make a flexible column that allows us to twist around, bend backwards and forwards, and from side to side. When we stand normally, the spine curves gently in and out, to absorb shock, increase its strength and ensure that the body weight is evenly distributed.

This X-ray shows some of the vertebrae that make up the spine.

The vertebral column

The vertebrae can be thought of in separate groups:

- **cervical:** the top seven vertebrae make up the neck. The first vertebra (the 'atlas') supports the head, and the joint between the atlas and the skull allows the head to nod up and down. The pivot joint between the atlas and the second vertebra (the 'axis') allows the head to turn from side to side.
- **thoracic:** the next twelve vertebrae form the back of the chest. These increase in size as they go downwards. Each thoracic vertebra is attached to a pair of ribs.
- **lumbar:** the five lumbar vertebrae are the biggest and strongest. They lie between the chest and the **pelvic girdle**, and they support the powerful muscles of the lower back.
- **sacral:** the five sacral vertebrae are separate in children but gradually fuse together between the ages of 16 and 30 to make one strong, curved bone – the sacrum. This adds strength to the pelvic girdle and helps to keep it stable.
- **coccyx:** the last three, four or five vertebrae also fuse together to make the coccyx, a tiny tail bone at the base of the spine.

What is a vertebra like?

Although each vertebra is different, they all follow the same basic design. The 'body' is the solid front (ventral) part of a vertebra. It faces inwards, and it is this part that carries the weight of the rest of the body.

Seven pieces of bone, called 'processes', jut out of the back (dorsal) and sides of the vertebral body. The two transverse processes are the sites where muscles are attached. The five articular processes link directly to the vertebrae above and below, stopping the vertebra slipping out of position.

Together, these pieces form a bony ring, with the body of the vertebra at the front and the other pieces of bone arranged into the vertebral arch.

Protecting nerves

When the vertebrae are stacked one on top of the other, the individual bony rings line up to make a hollow column. The spinal cord is a bundle of nerves running through this channel from the base of the vertebral column to the brain. Nerves run from the body, in between the vertebrae and connect with the spinal cord. The spinal cord is vitally important, carrying messages to and from the brain and every part of the body. Damage to the spinal cord can result in **paralysis** and loss of function, and so the protection offered by the bony column of the spine is extremely important.

Discs

Between each of the vertebrae is a disc of **cartilage**. The discs act as cushions to absorb shock. They also allow movement, and protect the bones by stopping the vertebrae rubbing together.

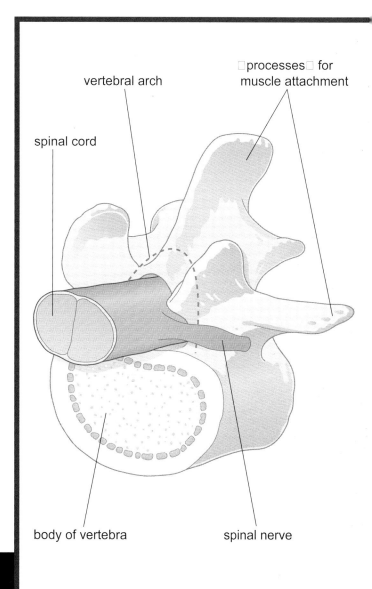

vertebral arch

processes for muscle attachment

spinal cord

body of vertebra

spinal nerve

This picture shows the structure of one vertebra. You can see the space through which the spinal cord passes.

Our spines allows us to carry out a wide range of activities, yet many of the things people do every day may be damaging their spines without their realizing. The information on this page may help you to look after your spine.

Carrying

The natural curves of the spine balance the body evenly, keeping the hips and shoulders more or less horizontal and making sure the weight is evenly distributed.

heavy bag in one hand – pectoral girdle unbalanced

pectoral girdle balanced by smaller bags in two hands or central bag

bending back to lift – strain on spine

bending at hips and knees keeps spine straight

slouching in chair – strain on spine

sitting straight – no strain on spine

special stool pushes weight onto knees – eases strain on spine

These diagrams show some ways in which you can help look after your spine.

Carrying a heavy bag on one shoulder, or in one hand, can completely distort this balance. The weight pulls down on one side and the other side rises to compensate.

You can avoid this happening, yet still carry the same weight, either by sharing the load between two smaller bags, one for each hand, or by carrying it all in one central bag like a rucksack. The rucksack must be worn properly, with a strap over each shoulder, to distribute the weight evenly over both shoulders.

Bending and lifting

If you curve your spine to reach down to pick up an object, you put a tremendous strain on it. A much better way is to bend your hips and knees, and pick the object up with your spine as straight as possible, minimising the strain on it.

Posture

We all lounge lazily in a chair sometimes, but this puts quite a strain on your **lumbar vertebra**. It really is not a good idea to sit like this regularly and for long periods. Try to sit well back into your chair, with your spine as vertical as possible, so you are sitting on your bottom and not on your lower spine.

Hunching over a desk can make your shoulders ache – and it is not good for your spine. Try to sit with your back straight; some office chairs are specially designed to take the strain off the back by spreading some of it to your knees.

Sport and spines

Some sports demand a lot more of the spine than others. Weightlifters usually wear a strong belt to provide extra support for their lumbar vertebrae. Some cricketers wear special corsets to avoid the spinal problems that years of bowling can create.

Warming up before you begin an activity is just as important for your spine as it is for other muscles and bones. Slow, gentle stretching movements can help to prevent strains and other injuries.

SPINAL PROBLEMS AND INJURIES

The spine is such a complex set of bones, bearing the whole weight of the body that it is hardly surprising that injuries occur. Some are bone problems, but many backaches are due mainly to muscular strain and do not directly involve any bones.

This person is wearing a neck brace to support their neck while they recover from a spine injury.

Slipped disc

Between each **vertebra** is a disc of **cartilage** that acts as a shock absorber and cushion. Normally, the weight of the body pulls down evenly, squashing the discs evenly. If the weight is uneven, as in carrying a heavy weight on one side, or bending a long way to one side, the discs will be squashed unevenly. Part of a disc may jut out past the vertebral column – this is known as a 'slipped' disc. If this presses on one of the spinal nerves, it can be extremely painful.

The treatment for a slipped disc depends on the extent of the injury. It may be enough simply to rest in bed, or gentle exercise and heat treatment may help. Traction, using a system of weights and pulleys, may be used to exert pulling forces on the spine to alleviate the problem. If the disc is badly damaged, an operation may be necessary to remove it completely and fuse the vertebrae together.

Broken back

The real danger of a 'broken back', or 'broken neck' is damage to the **spinal cord**. There are two main types of spinal **fracture**:
- compression fractures, where the body of one or more vertebrae is crushed. If the damage is limited to the body, and the vertebral arch is intact, the spinal cord will probably not be damaged.
- extension fractures, where the spine is pulled and stretched. An example of this is a severe whiplash injury that may be sustained in a car crash, or a horse-riding fall. The neck is forced backwards, the atlas vertebra breaks and part of the axis may even be snapped. A great force can separate the skull and these two vertebrae from the rest of the spine, and may break the spinal cord.

If the spinal cord is not damaged, support may be given with a neck collar or brace. If the spinal cord is damaged, the signals along nerves to and from the brain will be interrupted which may result in varying degrees of **paralysis** that will require long term treatment and care.

Unusual curves

A normal spine is gently curved, but some people suffer from slightly different spinal curves.

The most common is a scoliosis, where the spine curves from one side to the other, giving a twisted appearance. Much rarer is a kyphosis, where the **thoracic** vertebrae are more curved than usual, giving a humped back. Lordosis, where the **lumbar** region curves forward more than usual, is also uncommon.

This X-ray shows the curvature of a spine affected by scoliosis.

Some babies may be born with these curvatures, in some people they may develop as part of the aging process, poor posture or obesity, and in others they may be caused by diseases such as tuberculosis (which leads to degeneration of the vertebrae) or rickets (in which the bones do not form properly).

Spina bifida

During the months before birth, the vertebral arches are open, but they gradually close around the spinal cord, enclosing it completely. In babies with spina bifida, the vertebral arches do not all close completely, so that the baby is born with part of the spinal cord jutting out through the skin, covered with just a thin **membrane**. This means that the spinal cord, the vital bundle of nerves that is usually protected by the spine, could easily be damaged or infected. In some babies with spina bifida, surgery may be carried out to close the gap. In others, healing may occur naturally during the first few months of life. However, many babies born with spina bifida do not survive very long. There is evidence to suggest that a mother taking folic acid tablets during early pregnancy significantly reduces the risk of her baby having spina bifida.

The 22 bones of the skull form a bony shell that protects the brain, eyes and ears. They are all fixed together except for the lower jawbone, which is held in place by strong muscles. The skull bones are usually thought of in two sets – the cranial bones that make up the rounded, hollow part of the head, and the facial bones that make up the face.

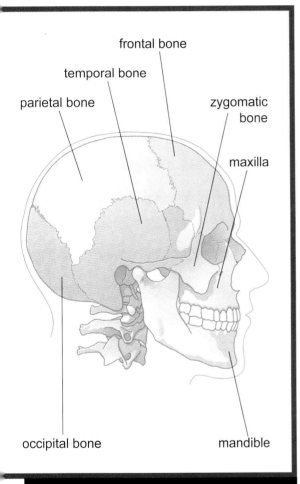

frontal bone
temporal bone
parietal bone
zygomatic bone
maxilla
occipital bone
mandible

These pictures show how the cranial and facial bones fit together.

Cranial bones

There are eight cranial bones, all joined together like a complicated jigsaw puzzle. The zigzag shapes of some of the bones means that they fit very tightly together. The joints between them, called sutures, are fixed joints, knitted together by strong fibres. Small, irregular sutural bones may occur between the sutures.

The cranial bones are:
- one frontal bone – its domed shape makes the shell of the forehead and the tops of the eye sockets
- two parietal bones – form the top of the head and the sides above the ears
- occipital bone – forms the lower back part of the **cranium**
- two temporal bones – at each side, behind the ears
- sphenoid bone – shaped like a bat with its wings stretched out, this bone lies in front of the ears and stretches right across the inside of the head from one side to the other. It helps to hold all the other cranial bones together.
- ethmoid bone – forms the roof of the nasal cavity and other internal parts of the head.

Facial bones

There are fourteen irregular facial bones. The picture shows how they all fit together to make the complex shape of the face.

The most obvious bones are the zygomatic bones (cheekbones), the nasal bones that form the bridge of the nose and the maxillae (upper jawbones).

The lower mandible (jawbone) is the largest and strongest facial bone. It forms a loose hinge with part of the temporal bones, and can move up and down, from side to side and backwards and forwards.

Sinuses

Some of the cranial and facial bones close to the nasal cavity have hollow spaces inside them called **sinuses**. These are lined with a mucus-producing **membrane**, and drain into the nasal cavity. They act as resonating spaces, amplifying sounds when we talk and sing. **Inflammation**, usually due to an infection or an allergic reaction, is called sinusitis. It can cause a build up of pressure inside the sinuses, and lead to a bad headache.

Fontanelles

The skeleton of a newborn baby is soft and delicate. Gradually **minerals** are laid down, and the bones harden and become stronger.

At birth, there are small spaces between the cranial bones, just covered by membranes and skin, that allow the skull to change its size and shape during birth. They will eventually be the sites of the suture joints, but until the bones harden and fuse they are very vulnerable. They are called 'soft spots', or fontanelles.

The baby in this photograph has a cleft lip.

Cleft palate and cleft lip

Usually, the maxillary bones that form the upper jaw of the face join before a baby is born. Sometimes, though, they are not properly joined at birth. The baby has a cleft palate or a cleft lip that may affect speech and swallowing. A cleft lip is usually closed surgically just a few weeks after birth. A cleft palate is usually closed between the ages of twelve and eighteen months, before the baby starts to talk. **Speech therapy** may be needed, but the results are usually very good.

The ribcage is made up of the ribs, the sternum (breastbone) and the **thoracic vertebrae**. It forms a bony cage, enclosing and protecting the heart and lungs. Its flexibility allows the chest to expand and contract as we breathe in and out.

The ribcage encloses and protects the heart and lungs.

Sternum

This is a flat, dagger-shaped bone about 15 centimetres long and 4 centimetres wide. It forms the centre of the chest, and provides anchorage for the ribs. It has three sections:

- a squarish upper section, with a notch on each side for the clavicles (collar bones) to attach to. The top pair of ribs is attached to this section, and the second pair are attached at the point where this section meets the middle section.
- a long middle section, to which the rest of the ribs are attached
- a small, pointed lower section that does not change from **cartilage** into hardened bone until the age of about 40. It provides anchorage for some major muscles.

Ribs

Most people have twelve pairs of ribs. Each rib is a flat bone, curved and slightly twisted into a flattened half-circle shape. Each rib is linked at a joint to a thoracic vertebra at the back. The top seven pairs are joined to the **sternum** by strips of cartilage. The next three pairs are linked together by strips of cartilage, and this joins the cartilage of the seventh pair to link on to the sternum. The last two pairs are called 'floating ribs' – they are not anchored to the sternum at all.

Each rib is linked to the ones above and below it by muscles that lie in the '**intercostal**' spaces between them. When these muscles contract, the ribs are moved upwards and outwards, expanding the chest space so that we can breathe in. When these muscles relax, the ribs move inwards and downwards, the chest space contracts and we breathe out.

In order to perform chest surgery, such as a heart transplant, doctors must use a metal retractor to keep the ribs apart.

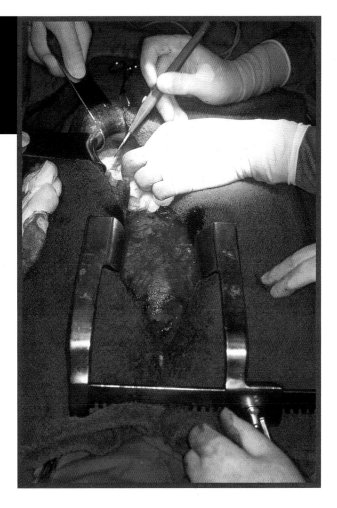

Broken ribs

A broken rib is the most common chest injury. It is usually the result of falling heavily, a direct blow, such as being thrust against the steering wheel in a car accident, or being crushed, such as a horse landing on its rider.

The ribs tend to break at the point where the greatest force is applied – in other words, where the chest was hit. They may also break at their weakest point, which is at the middle of the half circle shape where they are most curved.

Broken ribs may be very painful, but are not in themselves dangerous. However, they can lead to more serious injury if one of the **fractured** pieces damages internal organs such as the heart, lungs, liver or **spleen**.

In many cases, cracked and broken ribs may be left to heal by themselves, possibly with strapping around the chest to prevent further damage. In more serious cases, an operation may be necessary.

Chest surgery

If a patient needs a chest operation, such as heart surgery, doctors have to find a way to get inside the ribcage. They may do this by using a special clamp called a retractor to hold the ribs apart, and enter through the side of the ribcage. Alternatively, they may split the sternum down the middle to open the ribcage from above. The sternum can be stitched or stapled back together after the operation.

Our shoulder blades and collarbones form a horizontal crossbar to which our arms are attached. The shoulder joint allows the upper arm to move freely in any direction. We are able to use our arms and hands to do a wide variety of different things such as picking up heavy objects, throwing things, holding on to things and making tiny, precise movements.

This X-ray shows the bones of the finger and thumb forming an 'O'. This allows us to carry out tiny, precise movements, and is unique to humans and some other primates.

Pectoral girdle

The **scapulae** (shoulder blades) and **clavicles** (collarbones) together form the pectoral girdle. The clavicles are joined one to each side of the **sternum**. The shoulder blades do not join on to each other, or on to the **vertebrae**. Instead, they are held in place by a complex arrangement of powerful muscles and **ligaments**.

Upper arm

The upper arm consists of a single bone, the **humerus**, which moves freely in the ball and socket joint with the scapula. The shaft of the humerus is roughly cylindrical, widening at the bottom into a broad, flattened triangular shape to form the top part of the elbow joint.

Elbow joint

The elbow joint is a simple hinge joint, where the humerus meets the bones of the lower arm. It allows us to bend and straighten the arm. Overuse of this joint can result in swelling and tenderness, a condition known as 'tennis elbow'.

Lower arm

There are two bones in the lower arm – the radius and the ulna. The ulna is larger than the radius, and runs from the elbow to the outside of the wrist. The smaller radius runs from the elbow to the thumb side of the wrist. The radius and ulna meet at pivot joints at the elbow and wrist.

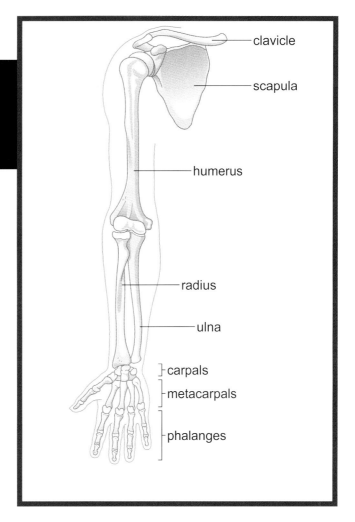

The radius and ulna are connected by strong fibres that lie in the space between them. These fibres allow the two bones to roll over each other so that we can turn our hands over from palm down to palm up and back again.

Wrist

There are eight small bones, the carpals, in each wrist, arranged in two rows of four bones each, joined together by ligaments. The gliding joints allow the bones to slide smoothly over each other, giving the wrist its suppleness.

Hand

The flat part of the hand is made up of five long thin bones, the metacarpals. These are linked directly to the finger bones, the phalanges. Each finger has three phalanges, but the thumb has only two.

We can move each finger bone up and down, bending our fingers. The special saddle joint between the first bone of the thumb and the metacarpal allows us to move the thumb in every direction.

Carpal tunnel syndrome

The carpal bones, together with fibrous **tissue**, make a channel called the 'carpal tunnel' through which a bundle of long **tendons** and nerves run. If this becomes inflamed, the nerves can get squashed, causing pain and tingling, and making it hard to carry out small, delicate movements. This is carpal tunnel syndrome, and is most common in people who use their fingers a lot, for example, computer terminal operators. Treatment is usually by rest and anti-inflammatory drugs, although an operation may sometimes be necessary.

The structure of the leg and foot is similar to that of the arm and hand. The **pelvic girdle** provides a horizontal crossbar to which the legs are attached at the hip joints. The bones of the legs are very strong, as they have to carry the weight of the whole body. The feet are flexible, allowing us to walk, run and jump.

When we walk, muscles pull the bones in a carefully co-ordinated sequence.

Pelvic girdle

The pelvic girdle is made up from the hip bones, the **sacrum** and the **coccyx**. The hip bones are the broadest bones in the body, and are made up from three smaller bones – the ilium, ischium and pubis, which fuse together between the ages of 15 and 18. The pelvis provides attachment sites for large muscles and for the legs, and allows the transfer of weight between the legs and spine. It also supports and protects organs in the lower abdomen.

There are important differences between the pelvic girdles of men and women. A man's pelvis is larger than that of a woman, and is rounder. A woman's pelvis is wider and shallower, allowing a baby to pass through when it is born. These differences are valuable in helping archaeologists determine the sex of ancient skeletons.

Thigh

The thigh has a single bone, the **femur**. This is the heaviest, longest and strongest bone in the human body. It is usually roughly one quarter of the full height of an adult. It is attached to the pelvis by the ball and socket joint at the hip. The joint allows movement in all directions, but the extent of movement is strictly limited by very strong **ligaments** to prevent **dislocation**.

Knee joint

The thigh and lower leg join at the knee. It is a hinge joint that allows us to move the lower leg to and fro. A sesamoid bone, the patella (kneecap), lies at the front of the knee joint.

Lower leg

There are two bones in the lower leg, the **tibia** and the **fibula**. They are connected by strong fibres that allow the bones to rotate around each other. The tibia, on the inside of the leg, is the larger and stronger of the two bones, and supports the body weight. The smaller, weaker fibula, on the outside of the leg, takes little of the body weight but it does give strength to the ankle joint.

Foot

The tibia and fibula meet the talus (ankle bone) at a hinge joint at the top of the foot. The talus fits into the calcaneus (heel bone), which lies underneath it and supports it. Together with five more bones, the tarsals, these take the weight of the body. The talus acts as a lever, with major muscles attached to it via the Achilles tendon.

The long central part of the foot is made up from five metatarsal bones, and these are attached to the phalanges (toe bones). The arrangement of bones is similar to that in the hands, but the bones are more restricted and have much less freedom of movement than in the hand.

Flat feet

If the ligaments in the foot are weak, the bones may move apart. The talus drops down into the space, and the shape of the arch collapses. This can usually be corrected by wearing a specially shaped insert (an orthotic) inside the shoe to support the bones.

Healthy bones

The bones of your legs and feet support the rest of your body, and allow you to move around. As with the other bones in your body, you can help to keep them strong and healthy by exercising and eating a healthy diet. Protecting bones makes sense too; wearing leg pads for sports like cricket and hockey can help to avoid injuries.

Shock absorbers

The tarsals and metatarsals are arranged in the shape of an arch, keeping us stable when we stand. This arch also allows the foot to absorb shock when we walk and run. A running step may flatten the arch by 1–2 centimetres, but it springs back into shape when the pressure is released.

WHAT CAN GO WRONG WITH MY BONES?

This book has explained the different parts of the human skeleton, why it is important and how it can be damaged by injury and illness. This page summarizes some of the problems that can affect young people. It also gives you information about how each problem is treated.

Many problems can also be avoided by good health behaviour. This is called prevention. Taking regular exercise and getting plenty of rest are important, as is eating a balanced diet. This is important in your teenage years, when your body is still developing. The table, which follows, tells you some of the ways you can prevent injury and illness.

Remember, if you think something is wrong with your body, you should always talk to a trained medical professional, like a doctor or school nurse. Regular medical check-ups are an important part of maintaining a healthy body.

Illness or injury	Cause	Symptoms	Prevention	Treatment
Stress fracture of the shin bones	A repeated action that puts too much strain on particular bones. Running on a hard road can put pressure on the shin bones (tibia).	Sharp pain in the shin. This can often be confused with shin splints, a pain in the shin that has similar causes but is less serious.	Good training shoes that cushion the legs and prevent too much stress on the shins. The shoes that protect your shins best may not be the most expensive or fashionable ones.	The main treatment is to rest the affected area until the fracture has healed, which can take months. Take exercise that doesn't put weight on the area, like swimming.
Rickets	Lack of vitamin D or calcium in the diet, which prevents new bone tissue being made.	Bones become weak, which causes them to bend, for example leg bones become bent.	Make sure you are eating the right things. Calcium and vitamin D are both found in milk and other dairy products.	Change of diet to include more calcium and vitamin D.

Illness or injury	Cause	Symptoms	Prevention	Treatment
Sprained joints	Joint gets overstretched or twisted too far, for example, if you trip over and twist an ankle.	Joint is sore and you are unable to put pressure on it, for example by walking.	Many joint problems can be prevented by warming up properly before exercising.	The joint needs to be rested, preferably in a raised position. Ice will help to reduce swelling.
Osteoarthritis	Cartilage that cushions joints is worn away and not replaced. Main cause in young people is when joints, which are still developing, are over-exercised or someone continues to play sport when injured.	Joints are very painful when moved.	Don't push your body too hard. When your body is still developing it is vulnerable when you put too much strain on joints like your knee joints. Don't use anabolic steroids.	Medicines may be given to reduce inflammation. Rest followed by physiotherapy can help to strengthen damaged joints.
Spinal problems and back pain	Can be caused by poor posture when standing or sitting. Also by lifting heavy objects and by carrying unbalanced loads.	Muscle aches and weakened ligaments, for example in legs. In severe cases, the spine can become unusually curved.	Stand up straight with weight distributed equally over both feet. Sit up straight in front of the TV or computer. Bend at the knees when lifting heavy objects.	Improved posture and exercise. Careful lifting and carrying.

Further reading

Horrible Science, Blood, Bones and Body Bits, Nick Arnold, Tony de Saules (Scholastic Hippo, 1996);
The Human Machine, Movers and Shapers: All about your muscles and bones, Sarah Angliss, Graham Rosewarne (Illustrator) (Belitha Press, 1999);
Human Physiology and Health, David Wright (Heinemann Educational, 2000);
Look at Your Body, Skeleton, Steve Parker (Franklin Watts, 1996)

GLOSSARY

antibiotics drugs used to fight infections. They destroy micro-organisms such as bacteria or fungi but are not effective against viruses.

bacteria type of micro-organism

bone marrow soft tissue at the centre of some bones, where blood cells may be produced and fat may be stored

bursa soft sac inside some joints that acts as a shock absorber

cancerous to do with cancer

cartilage strong, flexible material that protects bones

cervical to do with the neck

clavicle collar bone

coccyx tail bone

compact bone strong, hard material that forms part of a bone

cranium dome of skull

dislocate to move a bone out of its normal position

femur thigh bone

fibula shin bone (smaller)

fracture broken bone

friction force that occurs when two surfaces rub together

genes parts of every cell that contain genetic information

genetic passing of characteristics from one generation to the next

hormones chemicals made in the body. They travel around the body in the blood and affect organs and tissues in a variety of ways.

humerus upper arm bone

immune system the body's natural defence against disease and infection

inflammation swelling and tenderness of a joint or other tissue

intercostal between the ribs

ligament strong band of fibres that hold joints together

lumbar to do with the lower back

mass amount of material that something is made of

membrane thin covering layer of tissue

metacarpal hand bone

metatarsal foot bone

micro-organism tiny living thing that can only be seen under a microscope

mineral one of a number of chemicals needed by the body in small amounts

occupational therapist person who helps a patient to recover after injury or illness by using suitable exercises

orthopaedic branch of medicine specialising in bones and joints

ossicles one of the three tiny bones inside the ear

osteo to do with bones

osteoblast cell that is involved in formation of bone tissue

osteoclasts cell that breaks down bone tissue

osteocytes bone cells

paralysis inability to move part of the body

pectoral girdle scapulae and clavicles

pelvic girdle pelvis, sacrum and coccyx

phalanges bones of fingers and toes

protein complex chemical that is a component of many of the body's structures

radius lower arm (smaller bone)

rigid stiff and inflexible

sacral to do with the sacrum

sacrum vertebra forming back of pelvic girdle

scapula shoulder blade

sinus hollow space within a bone

speech therapy treatment to help people with speech and language problems

spinal cord bundle of nerves that runs within the spinal column

spleen large abdominal organ involved in the formation and destruction of blood cells

splint strong, rigid frame used to support and immobilise an injured bone

spongy bone mesh-like structure at the centre of some bones

sternum breast bone

steroids man-made drugs that are similar to some chemicals found naturally in the body

tarsal foot bone

tendon strong fibres that connect muscles to bones

thoracic to do with the chest

tibia shin bone (larger)

tissue different types of cell that work together to do one job

tumour swelling caused by abnormal growth of new cells

vertebra one of the bones of the spine

vitamin one of a number of chemicals that are needed by the body in very small amounts

INDEX